For

Elsie Natalie Brady
Alice Hansche Mortenson
Roxie Lusk Smith
With love and deep appreciation.

*You have helped
to light
The Candles of Hope
in so many lives
and you now share
in the Eternal Vision.*

"O Lord we crave for those gone home to Thee,
For those who made the earthly home so fair;
How little we may know, how little see
Only—that Thou art there . . ."

Salesian Missions wishes to extend special thanks and gratitude to our generous poet friends and to the publishers who have given us permission to reprint material included in this book. Every effort has been made to give proper acknowledgments. Any omissions or errors are deeply regretted, and the publisher, upon notification, will be pleased to make the necessary corrections in subsequent editions.

Copyright © 1991 by Salesian Missions, 2 Lefevre Lane, New Rochelle, N.Y. 10801

All Rights Reserved ©24879-I

First Edition in the U.S.A. by Concord Litho Co., Inc., Concord, N.H. 03301-0464

Candles of Hope

from the
Salesian Collection

Compiled and Edited
by Sara Tarascio

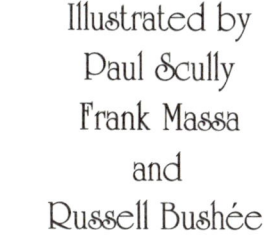

Illustrated by
Paul Scully
Frank Massa
and
Russell Bushée

CONTENTS

Old Things Are More Beautiful..7
Day in May 8
A Letter 10
There's Peace and Calm in the 23rd Psalm 11
My home to me... 12
God bless our home... 13
Trifles 14
A Candle 15
Give Me This Day...............16
All This and Heaven Too 17
An Autumn Day 18
God's Been Good to Me 19
My Treasures 20
A Passing of Days..............21
One by One 22
I am a Plowman 23
We always hope... 24
My Love For God 25
The Seeker 26
Quiet Days 28
Inventory 29
Ode to Spring 30
Walk in Faith 31
Little Things 32
As Close As My Back Door 33
A Walk To Yesteryear 34
The Gift 35
Welcome Friend 36
Pleasure Hunt 37

When Spring is in the Air 38
What More Than These 39
Precious Moments...............40
Harvest Time 41
The Singing Heart..............42
Life 43
My Window 44
Nature 45
True Wealth 46
Others 47
The Little World of Home.......48
Until This Hour 50
I Wish 51
My Hand in God's...............52
Autumn Pedestrian..............53
So Little Time 54
Troubled Waters 56
My Hope, My Strength, My Joy ..57
The Three Gifts 59
The Sunshine Breaks Through..60
Quiet Moments 61
O Lord, Thou knowest... 62
I Found the Wintertime 63
Sow and Reap 64
Unexpected Blessings 65
Lord, I Thank You..............66
Thank You 67
The Shepherd 68

Faithful Shepherd.....................69	My Treasures Are Secure........101
For Every Sorrow.....................70	The Miracle of Spring.............102
Prayer..72	Season of Rebirth....................103
Take Time 73	Great Faith That Smiles is Born of Great Trials............104
Reach Out 74	A Poet's Prayer 105
This Day....................................75	Gifts of Glory..........................106
Take Time 76	Treasures of the Heart.............107
A Peaceful Heart......................77	The crown of the house... 108
The Path of Life 78	The Sweetest Place 109
God's Joy 79	Lips of mine... 110
God in the morning... 80	A Recipe For Living 111
The Old Front Porch 81	The Homebody........................112
This Time of Year 82	Priceless 113
The Pilot...................................84	I Call it God 114
A Lighthouse............................85	A Walk on the Beach 115
Serenity 86	The Answer.............................116
The Goldsmith 87	Old Friends..............................117
Perhaps.....................................88	It's A Beautiful World.............118
Imagery 89	Make Me Worthy 119
Fellow Travelers 90	A Purpose For Trials...............120
Thank God for Little Things.....91	A Better Day 121
Symbols 92	The Gardener 122
A Yellow Daffodil....................93	My Search 123
A Balanced Life 94	The Tapestry 124
This Life Is What We Make It ..95	Thank You God... 125
Faith to See Me Through 96	Thank You for the Gifts 126
My Farm 97	Someone Cares 127
Show of Faith...........................99	A Candle Wish........................128
Living the Word 100	

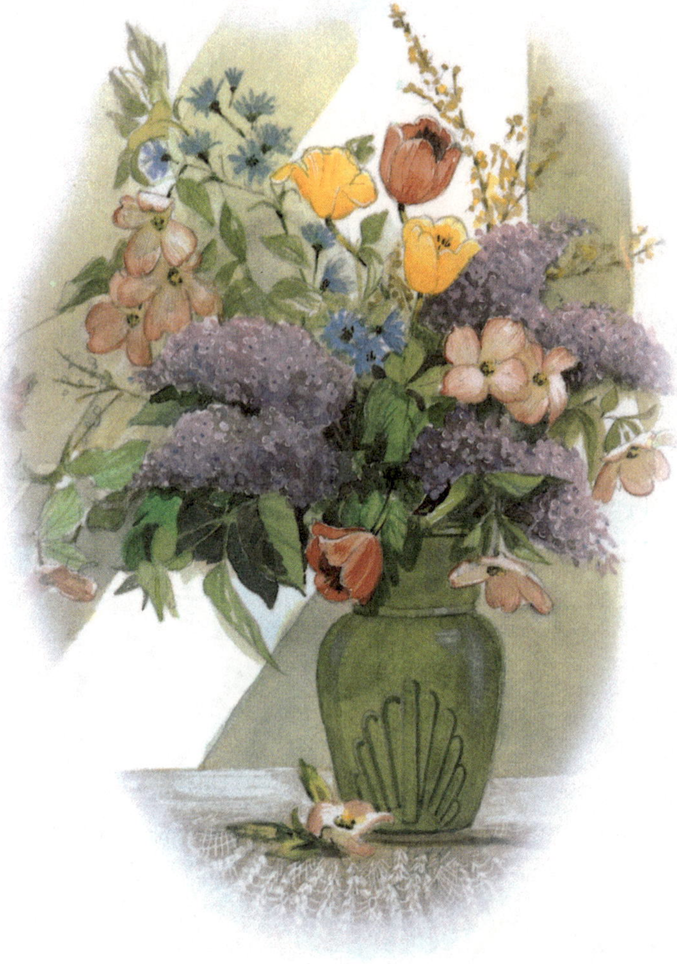

Old Things Are More Beautiful

Old things are more beautiful
    than many things brand new
Because they bring fond mem'ries
    of things we used to do.

Old photographs in albums,
    love letters tied with lace,
Recapture those old feelings
    that new ones can't replace.

Baby shoes, a teddy bear,
    a ring that grandma wore,
Are treasures waiting there behind
    a door marked "Nevermore."

Old things are more beautiful,
    more precious day by day,
Because they are the flowers
    we planted yesterday.

                Clay Harrison

Day in May

Many years ago, Dear Lord -
Upon this day, in May -
You willed me birth, upon this earth,
To live my chosen way
And in between - that day and now -
You watched me grow and sow
And seen and heard the words and deeds
I've spoken and bestowed.

You watched me revel, laugh and sing
Through happy years of life
And watched me cry - and heard me pray -
In times of grief and strife
But - always - You have only watched
And never curbed my ways.
You let me do what I would do
And say what I would say.

But Oh, my Lord, how much I wish
That You had stopped those deeds
That stained my soul with sin and shame,
In acts of lust and greed;
I wish that You had curbed each act
That haunts my mind today
For, now, I fear a sinner's doom
Upon my Judgment Day.

Yet such, I know, is not Your plan
For children on this earth
For, by Decree, You make us free
To prove our faith and worth
So I must, soon, come unto You
With sins of soul to pay
And hope I get a second chance
To live a better way.

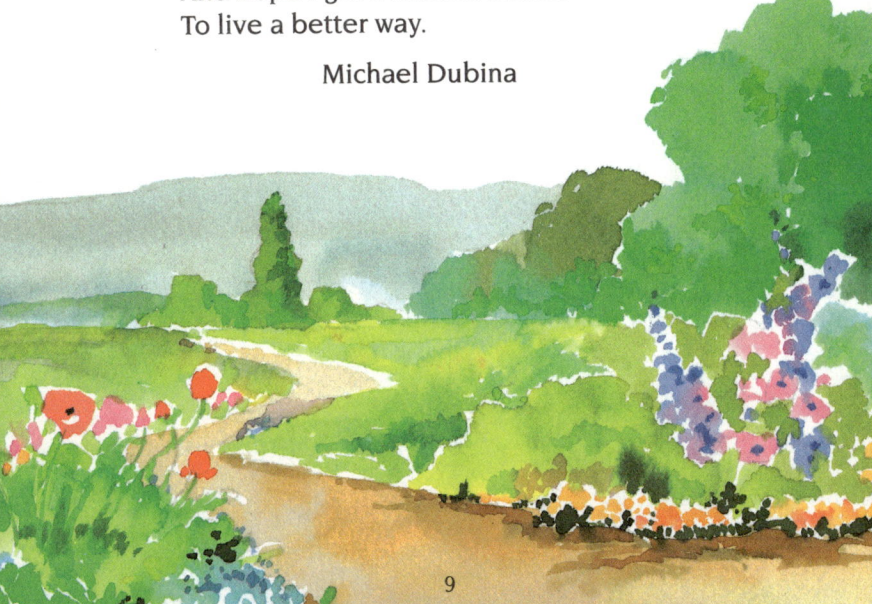

     Michael Dubina

A Letter

A letter is the warmest way
To bid a friend the time of day,
A keep-in-touch that brings the smiles,
Across the very longest miles.
And what a wealth of strength and hope,
Is tucked inside an envelope,
Reminding loved ones that you are,
At least in heart, not very far.

In no country, state or camp,
The wealth beneath a postage stamp,
For memories that never age,
Are written down upon each page.
And though it's nice to telephone,
One of the sweetest pleasures known,
Are moments shared in thoughts we send,
...That can be read, and read again.

Grace E. Easley

There's Peace and Calm in the 23rd Psalm

With the Lord as "your Shepherd"
    you have all that you need,
For, if you "follow in His footsteps"
    wherever He may lead,
He will guard and guide and keep you
    in His loving, watchful care
And, when traveling in "dark valleys,"
    "your Shepherd" will be there...
His goodness is unfailing,
    His kindness knows no end,
For the Lord is a "Good Shepherd"
    on whom you can depend...
So, when your heart is troubled,
    you'll find quiet peace and calm
If you open up the Bible
    and just read this treasured Psalm.

        Helen Steiner Rice

Used with permission of
The Helen Steiner Rice Foundation
Cincinnati, OH 45202

My home to me is hallowed ground
Where Paradise on earth is found.
Ardor and faith and joy divine
I pour into this task of mine
To make the home a place of joys,
To bless and guide my girls and boys,
Be inspiration, helper, friend,
To him whose fate with mine must blend–
what holier mission could there be?
My home is hallowed ground to me.

God bless our home, and help us
    To love each other true,
To make our home the kind of place
    Where everything we do
Is filled with love and kindness,
    A dwelling place for Thee,
And help us, God, each moment,
    To live most helpfully.

Trifles

Nothing so small that God has made
    But has its destined end,
All in their turn His purpose serve
    All to His glory tend.

The grain of dust, to sight unseen,
    With myriads may combine
To form a bulwark to the sea,
    Its limits to confine.

The little drop of pearly dew
    Which in the blue-bell lies,
May in the sun's bright beams appear
    A rainbow in the skies.

Or else the trackless ocean main,
    With others, form the share,
On which the ship, when homeward bound,
    Some loving heart shall bear.

And thus the humblest of us all
    God's instruments may prove,
To bless and shed o'er fallen men
    The bounty of His love!

A Candle

'Tis strange, that though a candle,
    And oh, so small it be;
The flickering flame it gives,
    In darkness, helps to see.

Its light dispels the darkness;
    The frightening shadows flee;
And all the fears of midnight,
    Are gone, when one can see.

The shadows crowd around one,
    And thunder roars above;
The fearful soul is drowning:
    He cannot see God's love.

My friend, you are a candle,
    And in God's plan, the light
That shines to those around you,
    To give the blind soul sight.

'Tis nice to be a lighthouse,
    To guide the ships at night,
But, friend, God needs the candles
    To give the lost soul light.

                Charles G. Ramsey

Give Me This Day

Give me this day, so beautifully good,
    Where the Master Himself, has painted the wood;
      Give me this day, its purpose to keep,
        To uplift my soul and let my heart speak.

      Give me this day, my hope to restore;
    Give me its silence, that I might hear more;
  Give me this day: renewal, release;
Proud in its challenge, strong in its peace.

Let my faith ride what fate has unfurled - - -
    Give me this day! Your gift to the world!
      Give me this day, a goal to achieve:
      And surely, my Lord,
          To not sit and grieve.

                Roxie Lusk Smith

All This and Heaven Too

He spread before us fertile land
    That we from it might eat;
He spoke and fountains opened wide,
    Our need for thirst did meet.

He spoke and trees did blossom forth,
    In strength and beauty stand
To spread their cooling shadow
    Throughout the grassy land.

God showed to us His tender love,
    Though barren, naked, we,
In that He gave to us His Son
    And through Him we are free.

Just thank Him now for everything,
    In love, He gives to you.
Just think He gave us everything
    And also Heaven too.

                Charles G. Ramsey

An Autumn Day

An autumn day is like a psalm of peace,
A whispered sigh, a half-forgotten smile,
The blending of a dozen different shades
Of gold and brown along each pensive mile.
A melody whose words the mind forgets,
Echoes through the rustling of the leaves,
Too deep to penetrate, the sacred hush,
Of moments such as these when one believes.

Standing on the threshold of the heart,
The scarlet maples flaming on a hill,
Recalling other hours long ago,
How can one bid such memories be still?
Something very wise and beautiful,
Lives in the yearly rendezvous of Fall,
A tangled trail . . . a puff of dandelion,
. . . One lone bird call.

        Grace E. Easley

God's Been Good to Me

I'm mindful of the blessings
  that come my way each day.
My heart is overflowing
  each time I kneel to pray.

I'm thankful for the seasons;
  each one's a masterpiece.
I'm allowed to work the land,
  but God still holds the lease.

I'm grateful for the friendships
  that brighten sorrow's way,
Because my cup of happiness
  sustains me every day.

I love the children and the flowers
  that decorate my life
And the quiet, gentle hours
  I spend with my wife.

I'm grateful for eyes that see
  the beauty of it all
Because God's been good to me
  and blessed me through it all.

I'm thankful for the little things
  that fill my life with love.
The best things in life are free;
  they come from God above!

Clay Harrison

My Treasures

Give me the simple things close to my home
    The things that are familiar, old and dear.
I do not have to wander far, or roam
    The Seven Seas, when I have splendor here.

Give me a crackling flame upon the grate
    And the warm smell of bread upon the fire.
I do not have to ride abroad in state
    To find the very core of heart's desire.

A shining tea-pot—friendly hands to pour
    And jam that smells of grapes from
        our own vine.
Could any noble king desire more?
    I am a king myself, for these are mine.

Let those who will seek promised lands afar,
    For treasures so remote I shed no tears.
Why should I strive to reach a distant star
    When heaven with all its beauty is right here!

A Passing of Days

Autumn leaves are lovely things,
    In shades of red and gold,
But they presage another time,
    When summer has grown old;
When frost paints crystal fantasies
    Upon the brown, bare hills,
That green in summer, freely spent,
    The gold of daffodils;
When brittle leaves in burning heaps,
    Perfume the keening breeze,
That searches aimlessly, a wraith,
    Among the tattered trees;
Unlike the autumn leaves that fall
    And sadly fade away,
Love blossoms brightly in the heart,
    To warm each passing day.

                Julie E. Jones

One by One

One by one, they lose their way
To the house in which I stay:
Friends and letters, dear to me;
Loves and fonds that used to be.
One by one, they disappear -
Like the joys of youthful years
That were roses on a vine -
Meant to fade to passing time.

Now, I must live on alone -
With the memories I own -
Learning that what used to be
Will, no longer, be for me.
Storms of life and aging time
Have destroyed each rose and vine
And, of friends - who used to be -
Only God is still with me.

                Michael Dubina

I am a Plowman

I am a plowman with a field,
    A furrow is my goal;
I look not to the job I've done
    Or job I've yet to do.

My eye is on the tree ahead
    To cut the furrow true:
My only goal, to finish first
    The job He gave to do.

Tomorrow or the years ahead,
    I ask not now to know;
I only ask to do the task,
    Whatever He may show.

"Dear Lord, I ask of Thee this day,
    Help me to plow for Thee,
To serve Thee where I am just now,
    To lead some soul to Thee."

                Charles G. Ramsey

We always hope; and
in all things it is
   better to hope
   than to despair.
When we return to
   real trust in God,
   there will no
   longer be room
   in our soul for fear.

   Goethe

My Love For God

If I could paint the beauty
That, God, I see in You,
My work would be a masterpiece
No artists could outdo.
No canvas ever could portray
The love within my heart,
For it is far too deep and great
For words to e'er impart.
Its magnitude goes far beyond
All else I ever knew.
There is no measure of the love
I have, dear God, for You.

     Harold F. Mohn

The Seeker

For many years I searched for God,
It seemed I could not find
His loving presence, vainly sought,
To give me peace of mind.

I followed blindly, many paths,
That led to grief and shame,
I tried to ease my conscience, when,
I'd call upon His name.

I knelt in chapels, great and small,
And sang sweet hymns of praise,
I begged forgiveness for my sins,
For peace to bless my days.

One day, I fed a hungry child,
And stilled its frightened cries,
I held it gently in my arms,
And wiped its tear-filled eyes.

I clothed an elder man, and gave
Him shelter from the cold,
The trembling smile upon his lips,
Was lovely to behold.

My questing heart was filled with joy,
I came to understand,
Each time I helped someone in need,
I touched the Master's Hand.

      Julie E. Jones

Quiet Days

Quiet days are precious gems
    Of treasured peace and calm,
No cares or troubles cloud the sky
    The silence is a balm.

My soul is soothed and worry free
    Such days in life are rare,
But when they come I feel God's love
    And know I'm in His care.

        Dolores Karides

Inventory

Have you ever taken stock
    Of things the Lord has done
By counting out your blessings
    And name them one by one.
The things we take for granted
    Would fill a lengthy list,
And maybe we'd stop complaining
    About little things we've missed.
Just count your answered prayers,
    And all the good times too.
Remember, too, the messengers
    And friends God sent to you.
And don't forget the miracles -
    I know you've had a few
When you climbed the highest mountains
    The world had given you.
The Lord was there to cheer you on
    When you had given up.
When your gas tank was on empty,
    He came to fill it up.
So often we don't thank Him
    For drink or daily bread,
And His Book there on the table
    Too often goes unread.
Examine us with mercy, Lord,
    When our hearts are too small
To comprehend Thy goodness, Lord...
    And forgive us one and all!

                Clay Harrison

Ode to Spring

Oh, how magical the Spring
And the joys that it can bring.
No other season can compare
To this happening so rare.

Flowers reaching for the sky,
Miracles we can't deny;
Woodland babes make their debut
And the world is fresh and new.

Feelings can't be put to words
As my heart soars with the birds.
I only know God loves us so,
To on us these gifts bestow.

    Catherine Janssen Irwin

Walk in Faith

I'll walk in faith with God today
    not knowing what it brings
I'll take each step that He directs
    and trust Him in all things.

I'll not lose hope if I am led
    in moments of despair
I'll lean on Him with all my might
    and trust me to His care.

I'll not assume that I know best
    if heartaches come my way,
Because He'll meet my every need
    I'll walk in faith today.

I'll take my walk in faith with God
    by every single minute,
And though my pathway be unknown
    by faith, I will walk in it.

He knows the road that I must take
    He knows each rock and stone
In faith I'll walk with God today
    I will not walk alone.

        Betty Purser Patten

Little Things

It's not the great things in this world
    that make our lives worthwhile,
It's the little things like a tiny flower
    or perhaps a baby's smile.
A little word, sincerely spoken,
    can lift our spirits high;
Like a tiny bird perched on a limb
    sends his message to the sky.
A little dew drop on a rose
    and tiny blades of grass,
All sparkle in the sunlight,
    to cheer us as we pass.
The lovely johnny jumpups,
    the smallest flower that grows,
Delight the heart of youngsters,
    peeping up around their toes.
A friendly gesture or a smile
    mean more to me than gold.
They help us feel that someone cares
    when we are growing old.
Money cannot buy the things
    that mean so much to me,
They are part of God's creation,
    and all of them are free.

              Laina Owen

As Close As My Back Door

Today God made a rainbow
Without a cloud in sight;
In fact, the sun was shining
And all the world was bright.
The lilacs bloomed profusely,
Perfuming all the air,
And there was bird rehearsal
With bird song everywhere.

Today God made a rainbow
In such a splendid way;
He fashioned it from sunbeams
And water that I sprayed.
For as I hosed the old back porch,
A humble, homely chore,
He made a lovely rainbow
As close as my back door.

     Loise Pinkerton Fritz

A Walk To Yesteryear

Come walk with me to yesteryear
Down the road of childhood miles,
Let's turn our thoughts away from fear
And change our frowns to smiles.

Let's walk together in memory
To times when we were young,
Let's live each minute in mimicry
And renew those years of fun.

     M. Rosser Lunsford

The Gift

It's true
We think about the rain
As dismal, darkened days,
    But look upon the sunshine
    As happy, brightened ways;

Yet, it really is the rain
Which brings us
All the things we need:
    The fruit, the food
    and all that grows, and
    The living seed.

So, when your days seem darkest,
And you feel a vague despair,
Recognize your rainy blessings
As a gift that makes life fair.

              Richard E. Paige

Welcome Friend

Welcome friend, how good of you to come,
What pleasant memories your face recalls.
Pull up a chair and let us sit and talk,
Stay long, for you bring sunlight to these walls.
Welcome friend, the pot is on the stove,
I'll set another place beside my own,
Forget your cares, remember two can share
A burden one could never bear alone.

Welcome friend, I say this from my heart,
You take away the chill of winter days.
I hear the warmth of springtime in your voice,
And after you have gone the wonder stays.
The fact that you have cared enough to come,
Means more to me than words can ever say.
The light of friendship glows within your eyes,
. . . And that is why I welcome you today.

                        Grace E. Easley

Pleasure Hunt

Who says there's nothing here to do
And life for them gets boring . . .
You'll never find me idle or
In bed just merely snoring.

> There's books to read and weeds to pull
> Flowers that need smelling . . .
> And roads to walk and streams to wade
> And stories that need telling.

There's friends to cheer, when life gets drear
And gardens that need hoeing . . .
Or take the boat down to the creek
To fish or go a-rowing.

> The song birds need a listening ear
> God's creatures need attention . . .
> Roll up your sleeves and go to work
> That will rid you of your tension.

      Lavonne Childers Minigh

When Spring is in the Air

It's a time for celebration
    When spring is in the air;
It's a time for exploration
    With flowers everywhere.

It's so good to be alive then
    When trees are born anew...
Such beauty stirs the hearts of men
    As dreams are coming true.

The earth is filled with sights and sounds
    So pleasing to our eyes
When miracles can be found
    Adrift in sunkist skies.

It's a time for celebration
    When spring is in the air:
It's a heavenly declaration
    That God is always there.

                Clay Harrison

What More Than These

A home that's filled with warmth and love,
A faith that's deep, in God above...
The song of birds at break of day,
The laughter of a child at play;
The joy that comes from tasks well done,
The gift of rest, at set of sun...
A shady tree, a bright blue sky,
A faithful dog, a friend nearby,
A rainbow shining after rain,
The twilight, music's sweet refrain;
Some favorite books, some wisdom learned,
And relaxation, rightly earned...
A glen where quiet rivers flow,
A dream that keeps one's heart aglow,
A flower garden, pink and white,
The blessings of good health and sight...
With these, and springtime at the door,
What man could ever ask for more!

                    Beverly J. Anderson

Precious Moments

Precious moments in my day, are -
   when I quietly slip away, and
Spend some time with my best Friend
   in moments I don't want to end.
Precious moments when I yield
   all of my being to His will,
Harried hours cease to be
   in moments with my God and me.
There's a peace this world can't bother
   in moments I spend with my Father.
My day just seems to shape-up right,
   my evenings turn to perfect night.
Precious moments go so fast -
   how I wish they'd last and last!
Yet, I know somehow they'll be
   moments in eternity.
So, I'll slip away this hour, for
   moments filled with mighty power,
For time more precious than pure gold
   in moments priceless to my soul.

            Betty Purser Patten

Harvest Time

There is so much beauty in living
But sometimes we miss the full glow,
Like the coral dawn in the morning
Like the whipped-cream clouds as they flow,
Like the rainbow ribbons in unison
Like the splendor of roses in bloom,
Like the diamond stars in full glitter
Like the blossoms midst fragrant perfume.
There is joy in the heart-beat of prayer
There's delight in the warm gentle rain,
There's His love spinning 'round us forever
And the joy of our faith to sustain.
There are dream seeds that need to be planted
And in due course the harvest will bring
A new dawn to greet your tomorrow,
A new heart with a spirit that sings.
So let us today plant a garden
In someone's heart and believe,
And as the result grow much richer
For we each shall partake and receive.

     Chris Zambernard

The Singing Heart

May you have a singing heart,
Whose tone is sweet and clear,
Living to the melody
You've learned to play by ear.
A happy and a hopeful heart,
Whose lyrics lightly lift
All sadness so that folks may share
The wonder of your gift.

May you have a singing heart,
Delighting to the sound
Of silver rounded notes that bear
Your feet above the ground.
A trusting and courageous heart,
Advancing through each measure,
A deeper and a richer soul,
Because of such a treasure.

              Grace E. Easley

Life

Life is a grand adventure
We live through day by day.
Life is truly a challenge
In every sense and way.

Life has its rays of sunshine
As well as dark clouds too.
Life is always uncertain
We learn each day anew.

Life is bestowed upon us
By that great King above.
Life to be lived its fullest
Must know His ways and love.

   Harold F. Mohn

My Window

As I gaze from my window
All His wonders I see
The soft summer breezes
Gently swaying the trees.

> Birds flit and flutter
> To and fro from their nest
> As they gather the food
> For their young ones at rest.

While off in the distance
The great mountains rise
Their peaks ever reaching
Almost touching the sky.

> The sounds of God's creatures
> Faintly fall on my ears,
> My emotions run rampant
> My eyes fill with tears.

Tears of joy, not of sorrow
That from my glass I see
All the beauties of nature
God bestowed upon me.

    Albert N. Theel

Nature

The beauty of God's Universe,
Is held in wonderment,
We never could produce it,
It must be heaven sent.

The sanctity of nature,
Is something to behold,
The changing of the seasons,
From warm to very cold.

The rain we call spring showers,
The wind that blows a breeze,
The autumn leaves of red and gold,
As they fall off the trees.

The vastness of the mountains,
Sun and clouds up in the sky,
Animals that roam the earth,
The majestic birds that fly.

Where do snowflakes come from?
Is there really a "dark hole?"
How do geese know where to fly,
Or the oceans where to roll?

Nature belongs to all of us,
Yes, to you and me,
And to think it costs us nothing,
It is absolutely free.

    Hope Ulch Brown

True Wealth

I am rich because I know the Lord,
    Not accumulated wealth...
I am rich because He blessed me
    With presumably good health...
I am rich because I have good friends,
    A family of my own...
I am rich because of shelter,
    A place which I call home...
I am rich because of angels
    Who guard me night and day...
I am rich because there's Someone
    To listen when I pray...
But most of all, I'm rich because
    He shed His blood for me...
And I shall dwell in the House of God
    For all eternity.

                Helen Parker

Others

Lord, help me live from day to day
    In such a self-forgetful way,
That even when I kneel to pray,
    My prayer shall be for "Others."

Help me in all the work I do,
    To ever be sincere and true,
And know that all I do for You
    Must needs be done for "Others."

Let self be crucified and slain
    And buried deep; and all in vain
May efforts be to rise again
    Unless to live for "Others."

And when my work on earth is done,
    And my new work in Heaven's begun,
May I forget the crown I've won,
    While thinking still of "Others."

"Others," Lord, yes, "Others !"
    Let this my motto be.
Help me to live for others,
    That I may live for Thee.

                Charles D. Meigs

The Little World of Home

There is a little world of home
Where loving hearts shall dwell;
'Tis here we find a beauty real
We know and love so well.
It demands the best within us,
For unless we here succeed,
We will ever be a failure
In all other words or deed.

Within our little world of home,
'Tis hard to be a saint,
For here is where we grumble most
And often voice complaint;
'Tis here we live and work and play,
Where life brings each new test,
The place where hopes and dreams are born
With those we love the best.

Oh, lovely little world of home,
Though trials may oft arise,
We find the miracles of life
Before our very eyes;
'Tis here success must surely come
If we'd succeed at all,
Within the arms of those they love,
So many rise or fall.

Rich thoughts are born, a courage real,
Perhaps a heartache too;
'Tis here we plan a way of life
And cherish dreams come true;
Sweet memories from childhood days
We treasure as our own,
And know that life is dearest in
The little world of home.

      Garnett Ann Schultz

Until This Hour

I view with so much sadness
So many days of past
I could have better done so much
That would much better last -
A lot of little, common things,
That came to pass, each day,
But never seemed to matter, much -
Until this hour, today.

So many simple, daily deeds,
I could have better done;
So many days I could have spent
In better loving, one;
And O' so many, many times
I could have better prayed
To show my Lord more lasting faith
For blessings of each day.

But these are hours and careless deeds
I cannot live, anew,
(To better gild, with lasting love,
The little things we do)
So, I must pray God understands
I rue my thoughtless ways -
But little things didn't matter, much -
Until this hour, today.

        Michael Dubina

I Wish

I wished the sun would always shine
And skies would not turn gray,
And life would be the way it was
When I knew how to play.

Each day was filled with happiness
A wonderment galore,
The beauty of each passing day
Concealed what lay in store.

As years went swiftly marching by
And troubles reared their head,
I found a Friend who taught me that
Life's trials I should not dread.

He said to bless our heavy loads
Accept them with a smile,
For He would give us strength to bear
And walk with us each mile.

I took Him at His promise,
By faith, He filled all lack,
I gave Him all my burdens,
And I don't ever want them back.

Now, all my days are sun filled
'Cause when the skies turn gray,
I call upon my new found Friend
To brighten up my day.

              Shirley R. Heinrich

My Hand in God's

Each morning when I wake I say
"I place my hand in God's today."
I know He'll walk close by my side,
My every wandering step to guide.

He leads me with the tenderest care
Where paths are dark and I despair,
No need for me to understand,
I but hold fast to His hand.

My hand in His. No surer way
To walk in safety through each day.
By His great bounty I am fed,
Warmed by His love, I am comforted.

When at day's end I seek my rest,
I realize how much I am blessed.
My thanks pour out to Him, and then
I place my hand in God's again.

     Lori Stanley Hamilton

Autumn Pedestrian

Where shall I walk this autumn day?
What shall I choose to do?
Oh, I shall wander a leafy way
beneath a comforting blue.

I shall hug with a longing gaze
each tree, each mellow leaf,
and wonder what lies in the distant haze
surrounding this afternoon brief.

I shall leave worries and cares behind,
taking along only praise;
this walk will be restful, and I will find
peace and strength for tomorrow's days.

Where shall I wander this leafy day,
and what shall I choose to do...
Oh, I shall walk an autumn way
and absorb an artist's view.

      Pollyanna Sedziol

So Little Time

So little time to say the things
You'd really like to say -
Before you even find the words,
The time just slips away.

So little time to do the things
You feel that you must do.
So treasure, like the purest gold,
The time God's given you.

So little time to dream your dreams,
For youth has passed its prime,
And all too soon you realize
That there's . . . so little time.

So little time to reach the height
To which you're bound to climb,
For swiftly pass the waning years,
And there's . . . so little time.

So little time for past regrets,
And less, to make amends,
Yet God can heal the deepest wounds
In chosen, cherished friends.

So little time to share God's love
And beauty here on earth,
And know, before His endless time,
Their meaning and true worth.

Oh, yes, there is so little time
To seek the hidden door
That opens up to heaven's time,
Where time's forevermore.

     Sister Miriam Barker

Troubled Waters

Is your head bowed down in sorrow,
As you come to the end of day,
Is there no one you can turn to,
And somewhere have you lost your way?
"Let not your heart be troubled,
Neither let it be afraid,"
Joys awaiting you tomorrow
Have merely been long delayed.
And whether you voice your problem,
Or just meet Him in silent prayer,
God hears and He oft times answers
In a way that we know He cares.
Come what may, you can endure it,
If you will pray your way through it.

      Laura Baker Haynes

John 15:27

My Hope, My Strength, My Joy

He sends to me a rainbow
  To help my sorrows mend,
When my body's sorely aching
  And my troubles know no end.

He lifts me up and carries me
  High above the storm,
That threatens to obscure my path
  When doubts and fears take form.

His merciful love enfolds me
  As I face the raging tide
That seeks to overturn the boat
  When mighty crests I ride.

His guidance helps me stay afloat
  Till I reach the distant shore,
Then leads me the way to soothing rest
  Beyond a friendly door.

          Catherine Janssen Irwin

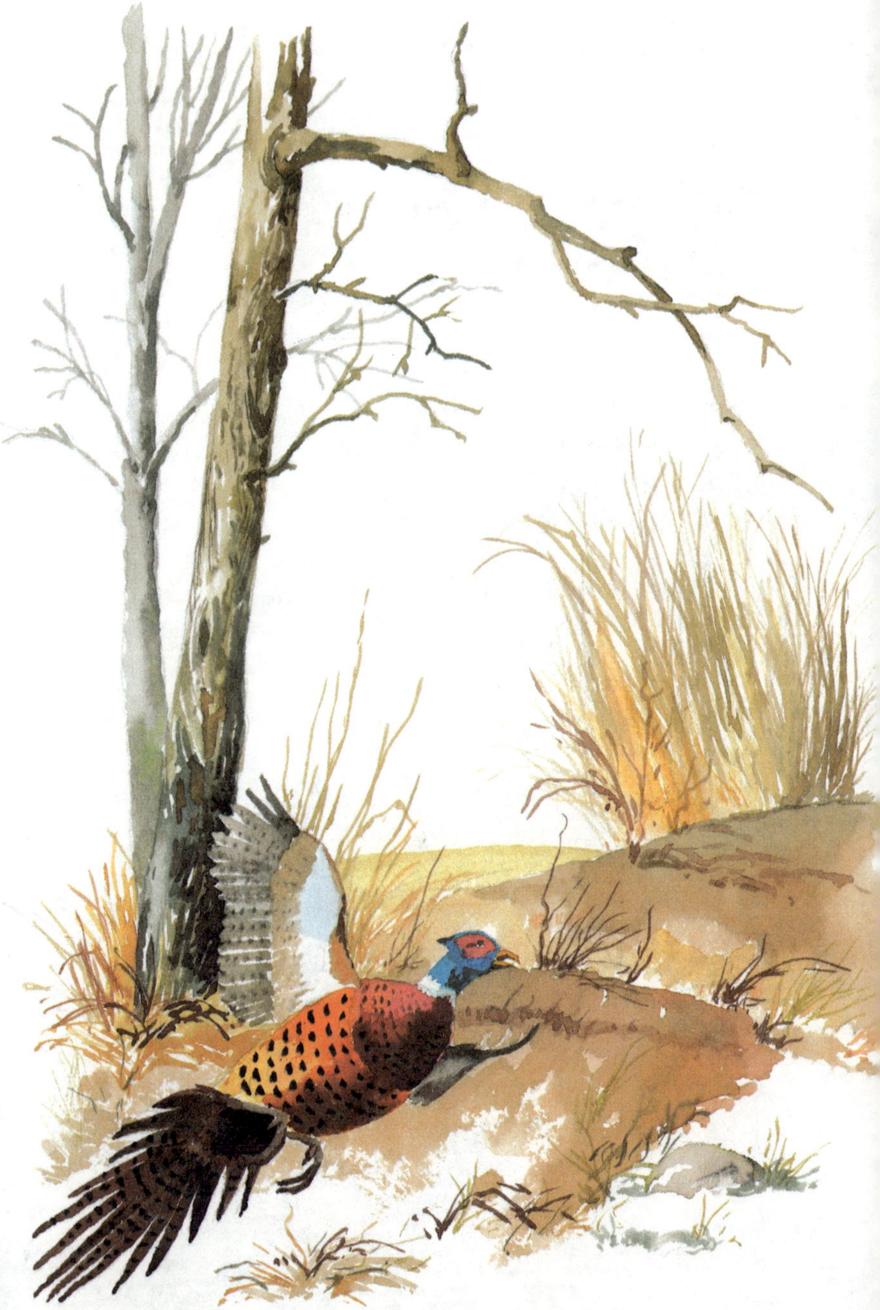

The Three Gifts

Faith, is the germ and seed,
Of intent, act and thought,
It goes before -- the soul doth feed;
And by it, noble things are wrought.

Hope is a window shining clear,
Giving vistas of beauty rare.
Keeping the heart from nameless fear,
And showing horizons, wondrous, fair.

Love is from God on high.
'Tis gentle, strong, patient-true --
It reaches unto the very sky;
It is holy, tender, and joyous too.

Faith -- hope -- love, a wise design
Are given our beings to refine,
To be more like our Master, day by day,
To aid and cheer a neighbor on his way.

Three noble gifts have come to man,
These are a part of God's great plan.
Sweet trilogy of gifts from above --
Faith -- hope, but greatest of all is love.

    David B. Achterkirch

The Sunshine Breaks Through

The day may be dreary
and the sky overcast
But I'm not concerned
that the climate will last.

For the love in my heart
and the warmth in my soul
Give me comfort and power
to banish the cold.

When my faith in the Lord
remains steadfast and true
Then into my life
the sunshine shines through.

And the light of the Lord
illumines the way
To change gloom into joy
and a bright cheery day.

    Dolores Karides

Quiet Moments

There's such pleasure in the silence
    of a summer afternoon,
And comfort in the shadows
    of a cozy, firelit room.

There is quality in hush of dawn
    when morning sunrays steal
Into the waning clouds of night,
    day's beauty to reveal.

In gentle moments such as these,
    I have scaled to heights above,
Felt winds of joy upon my face,
    and known the peace of love.

        Frankie Davis Oviatt

O Lord, Thou knowest well how dark the way,
Guide Thou my footsteps, lest they stray;
Give me fresh faith for every hour,
Lest I should ever doubt Thy power
And make complaint!

Give me a heart, O Lord, strong to endure,
Help me to keep it simple, pure,
Make me unselfish, helpful, true
In every act, whate'er I do,
And keep content.

Help me to do my share,
Make me courageous, strong to bear
Sunshine or shadow in my life!
Sustain me in the daily strife
To keep content!

I Found the Wintertime

I found the wintertime today
Along the wondrous autumn way.
The very lovely snowflakes white
Had softly fallen in the night;
Each naked branch now glistened fair
Within the frosty morning air.

How silent are the magic charms
As winter holds us in his arms,
An artistry just God can bring,
A miracle in everything.
So thick and deep snow's carpet lies
In wintertime's so sweet surprise.

The country lanes did bid me go
Into a world of sparkling snow,
A loveliness as yet untold
That glistened neath the sunshine gold
To ever thrill this heart of mine.
Today I found the wintertime.

    Garnett Ann Schultz

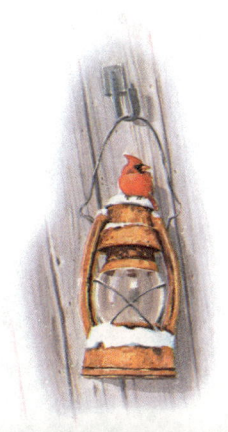

Sow and Reap

Send a loving letter
To a friend along the way,
And bring joy to another
With a "happy new today"...

Plant a rose of splendor
And nurture with delight
Then the beauty will keep
    blooming...
For all who come in sight.

Gather bits of wisdom
And scatter as you go,
Then you're bound to keep
    on reaping...
Just exactly what you sow.

        Chris Zambernard

Unexpected Blessings

Thank You, God, for little things
    that come unexpectedly
To brighten up a dreary day
    that dawned so dismally.
Thank You, God, for sending
    a happy thought my way
To blot out my depression
    on a disappointing day.
Oh, God, the list is endless
    of things to thank You for,
But I take them all for granted
    and unconsciously ignore
That everything I think or do,
    each movement that I make,
Each measured rhythmic heartbeat,
    each breath of life I take
Is something You have given me
    for which there is no way
For me in all my "smallness"
    to in any way repay.

        Helen Steiner Rice

Used with permission of
The Helen Steiner Rice Foundation
Cincinnati, OH 45202

Lord, I Thank You

Lord, I watched the dawn this morning
    As the sunlight filtered through,
And I thought about how Your love
    Streams from heaven and warms me, too.

Then I heard the birds sweet chorus
    And I thought about Your care.
For I know You watch the sparrow -
    When one falls You are aware.

As I gazed upon the flowers,
    Lord, I found Your peace was there.
Little flowers do not worry -
    They just rest within Your care.

Lord, I thank you for the beauty
    As I greeted this new day,
And especially for the lessons
    That You taught in Your Own way;

For the sun and birds and flowers
    Are reminders of Your care,
And of promise for provision
    To Your children everywhere.

        Beverly J. Anderson

Thank You

I thank You, God
  For little things,
    Happiness that
      Children bring . . .
        Fuzzy kittens,
          Soft to touch,
            Frisky puppies,
              Birds and such.

Clouds suspended
  In the sky
    Raindrops on the
      Meadow, dry . . .
        Freshened grasses
          Shrubs and trees,
            Flowers kissed
              By honey-bees.

Frozen droplets
  Cycled ice . . .
    Snowflakes on my
      Nose . . . oh, nice!
        I thank You, God,
          Each little thing
            Tells Your love,
              Makes my heart sing!

    Anna Lee Edwards McAlpin

O Lord, how manifold are Thy works!
In wisdom hast Thou made them all:
the earth is full of Thy riches.
    Psalm 104:24

The Shepherd

The Shepherd loves His sheep
    And wants them not to stray,
But their untamed nature
    Oft' leads them far away
To fields that promise pastures,
    Greener than their own,
Gleaning worldly tares,
    For which they must atone,
By giving up their temporal wants,
    Returning to the fold,
Of the loving Shepherd,
    Whose mercy is untold,
Forgiving every wayward sheep,
    No matter where they roam,
With love that is eternal,
    He welcomes them back home.

        Colette Fedor

Faithful Shepherd

From thoughtless words that I might say,
Seal my lips oh Lord I pray.
Let me, only kindness show
Everywhere I chance to go.
If beset with trial and care,
Strengthen me, that I might bear
Pain or sorrow patiently,
Placing all my trust in Thee.
Faithful Shepherd, lead the way,
Guide me through the coming day.
At eventide, send quiet rest
Wrapped in peace, by angels blest.

Elsie Natalie Brady

For Every Sorrow

For every sorrow You bestow,
You also send a sweetness.
Diluting each and every pain,
By Your dear Love's completeness.
You always keep reminding me,
As long as each man lives,
That while one hand may take away,
  . . . Your other always gives.

For every rock that cuts my foot,
You move a stone away,
And when life asks too much, You find
A price that I can pay.

When my cries are loudest,
And seem to no avail,
And walls rise up to block my path,
. . . You blaze another trail.

Each time my heart grows weary,
You send Your blessed peace,
And when my boat is tempest-tossed,
You bid the storm to cease.
So side by side we walk along,
My Lord and dearest Friend,
For every cross I carry,
. . . You lift the other end.

     Grace E. Easley

Prayer

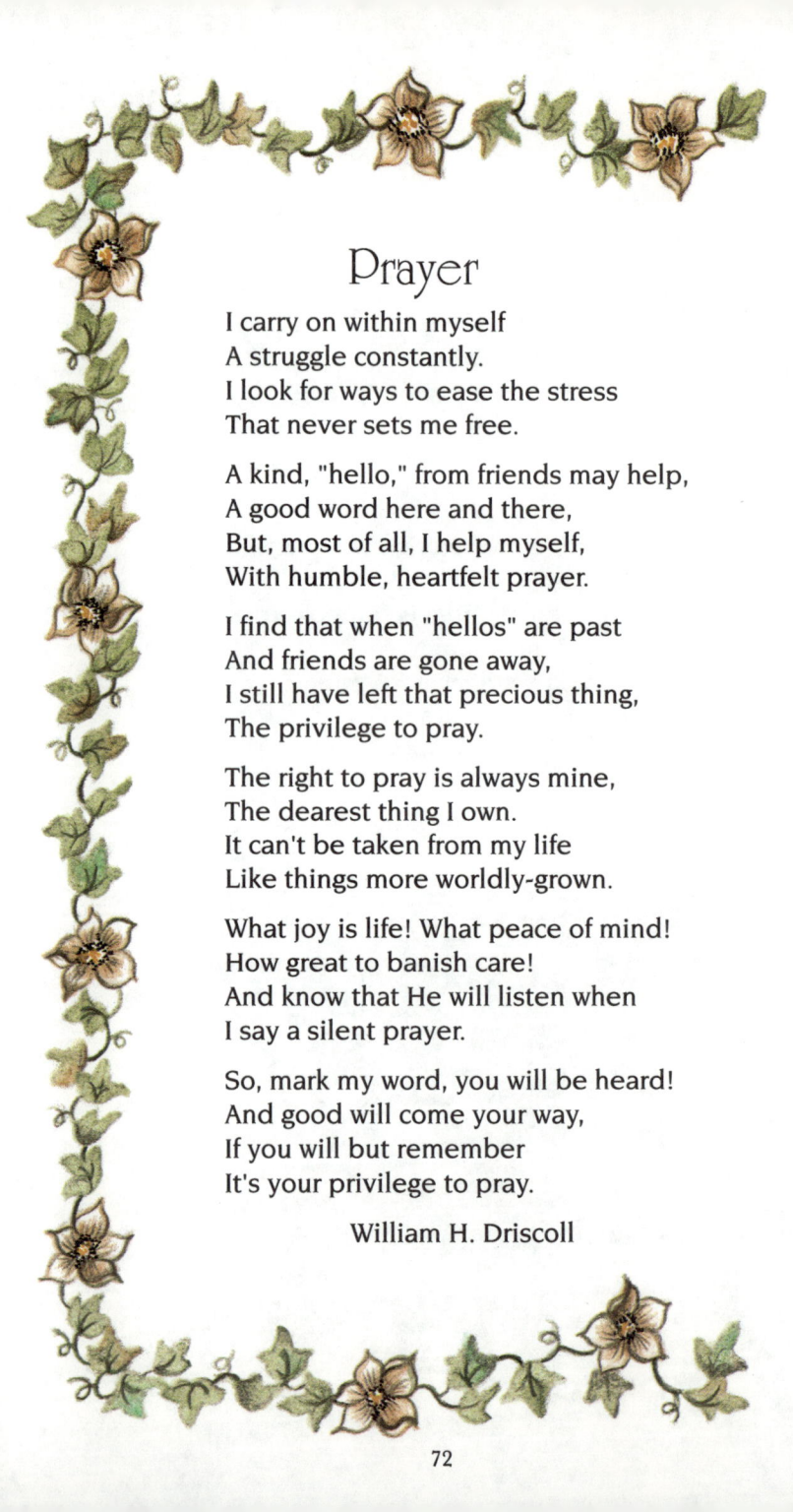

I carry on within myself
A struggle constantly.
I look for ways to ease the stress
That never sets me free.

A kind, "hello," from friends may help,
A good word here and there,
But, most of all, I help myself,
With humble, heartfelt prayer.

I find that when "hellos" are past
And friends are gone away,
I still have left that precious thing,
The privilege to pray.

The right to pray is always mine,
The dearest thing I own.
It can't be taken from my life
Like things more worldly-grown.

What joy is life! What peace of mind!
How great to banish care!
And know that He will listen when
I say a silent prayer.

So, mark my word, you will be heard!
And good will come your way,
If you will but remember
It's your privilege to pray.

    William H. Driscoll

Take Time

Life is so precious,
Don't waste a day!
Live life to the fullest
In small simple ways.
Take time, smell the roses.
Hear the song of a bird.
Take time, say, "I love you."
Three beautiful words!

Take time, watch the sunset
All pink, red and gold.
Take time and just stand still;
It's a sight to behold.
Take time, watch the moon rise
And spread its soft light.
You can feel God's sweet presence
In the still of the night.

Take time and just listen
And you'll hear Him say,
"I love you, my child
And I'm with you each day."
No more will we worry,
Our cares disappear
When we take time
And know God is near.

          Mary Ann Houston

Reach Out

Reach out to the aged,
add light to the eyes
of the bent and the stricken,
the sad, the unwise.

Whenever you can,
find something to share
with the homeless or lost ones
to show that you care.

For these children of God
are in need of a friend,
and the love that you give
is a love without end.

> Adele Kenny

This Day

Let us help a neighbor
Along his way today,
Give some thought and action
To things we do and say,
Show a true compassion
For those who have a need,
Fill the lonely hours
By doing a fine deed,
Help someone in sorrow,
Comfort with a prayer,
Help them in their heartache
To conquer and forbear,
Turn to God for guidance
Then be a friend to all,
For this day is rich with blessings
As we heed a higher call.

Virginia Borman Grimmer

Take Time

In the quiet time of evening
At the setting of the sun
Before the moon arises
And all the work is done
Take time to thank the Saviour
For the blessings of the day
And in the quiet stillness
Just fold your hands -- and pray.

        Betty Christman

A Peaceful Heart

With each and every fresh new day
May You guide my thoughts and deeds,
That I might be true to Your Will, Lord,
Forgetting my own selfish needs.

Then when I close my eyes in sleep
Please bid my fears depart -
And let me waken in the dawn
With a peaceful, happy heart.

              Dorothy Kohlberger

The Path of Life

When walking down the path of life,
    remember what I say,
that every man must feel the thorns
    that grow along the way.

And every soul will stumble,
    for every man is weak,
and the road of life uncertain,
    its prospects often bleak.

But always give a helping hand,
    a word of love, a smile,
to help the soul beside you walk
    across each weary mile.

For love will cause the sun to shine,
    and everywhere you go,
the painful thorns less noticed as
    the roses bloom and grow.

          Kate Watkins Furman

God's Joy

As God's great joy flows through us
    and makes our pathway bright,
Each day brings us rejoicing
    and reasons for delight.

Joy puts a smile upon each face,
    Its light glows in our eyes.
As we express God's joy we're blessed.
    We come to realize, -

God's joy within us is our strength,
    and we are strong.
God's joy within us is our peace,
    our joy, our song.
God's joy within us is our health,
    and we are whole,
For God has placed within our hearts
    the joy of His own soul!

Thank you, God, for Your great joy
    that blesses us so much.
May our lives' overflowing joy
    bless other lives we touch.

        Micky Meyer Mathewson

God in the morning,
   Peace for the day.
God at the noontide,
   Rest upon the way.
God in the evening,
   Will make the shadows flee.
God for all our lifetime,
   Is joy eternally!

       Dorothy A. Doane

The Old Front Porch

Our old front porch...I can see it still,
Just as it used to be,
Embracing the house at the foot of the hill,
Waiting for company.

It is older now, but yet as strong
As it was when we were young,
But the honeysuckle vines are gone
And the wind-chimes' tinkling song.

The porch was always a cheerful place,
With flowers and rocking chairs.
It had old-world charm, with handmade lace
Under vases and souvenirs.

Sometimes, we stop to visit awhile
With the folks now living there,
And the porch seems to greet us with a smile,
As happy memories we share.

   Elsie Natalie Brady

This Time of Year

There's a touch of sweet nostalgia,
About this time of year,
A whimsical illusiveness
That borders on the rare.
Each multicolored moment
Reflected through the screen
Of inner thoughts that brush the realm
Of sensed and yet unseen.

Crocheted across the countryside,
In intricate design,
An afghan made of silver frost,
By hands that are divine.

And through the woodland's manor,
Dispelling shadowed gloom,
Golden threads of sunlight
From the Master's busy loom.

Through the symphony of silence,
The wild geese overhead,
And in their throats a lyric
Such as man has never read.
And my humble heart is thankful
For this special time of year,
For no sermon any greater,
...Than these feathered wings I hear.

        Grace E. Easley

The Pilot

As you travel on life's ocean
    Are there storms that overwhelm?
And you think your ship is sinking.
    Let the Saviour take the helm.

Do you hear the tempest roaring,
    And the waves dash on the sea?
Pray, although your lips may tremble,
    "Jesus, Saviour, pilot me."

As the storm clouds ever darken
    And your Captain seems asleep,
Trust Him in the raging waters -
    He will save you from the deep.

Let Him only do the steering,
    Have no fear, He knows the way,
He will bring you safe to harbor,
    To the land of endless day.

There He will cast the anchor over
    Lead you gently to the shore.
All the storms of life forgotten -
    Blissful peace, forevermore.

                Martha Sanders

A Lighthouse

There stood upon an island bare,
    A lighthouse tall and strong;
That stood there 'gainst the stormy sea,
    Through many hours long.

We sailed the seas both far and wide,
    And oft' times passed this light;
That warned us from the rocky shore,
    And saved us from its plight.

How many times its light has warned,
    The many who passed there;
Who by its light, their course could tell,
    And miss the threatening snare.

There stood upon a window sill,
    A little candle bright;
That stood throughout the stormy night,
    And flickered forth its light.

I've travelled far around this world,
    But when I pass this light, -
It makes me think of those inside,
    Who give the wanderer sight.

The little candle stood alone,
    To tell to those who roam,
To show to wandering travellers far,
    A place that we call home.

A lighthouse or a candle,
    Is what I am for Him;
That gives its light to tell to all,
    How Jesus died for sin.

The lighthouse shines to many,
    The candle to a few;
A lighthouse or a candle,
    Is what He seeks in you.

        Charles G. Ramsey

Serenity

I looked across a quiet hill
And saw a tree of green,
A blue sky nestled overhead
A valley snug between.
My heart reached out to hold it fast
This wondrous work of God,
As silently I kneeled to pray
Upon the earth's green sod.

I looked beyond the quiet hill
And found a breeze at play,
A bit of gentle peacefulness
This more than lovely day.
A bird was calling to his mate
A beauty filled the air,
I saw the springtime budding forth
Around me everywhere.

I looked into a happy world
Where nature ruled supreme,
Beyond the realm of worldly cares
A quietness, serene -
And then I knew serenity
My heart knew joy and love,
I looked across a quiet hill
To heaven up above.

                Garnett Ann Schultz

The Goldsmith

The babbling brook
    flows cool and clear
It comes and goes
    I know not where

Polishing pebbles, rocks, and sand
While flowing through the thirsty land.

A glittering, shimmering piece of gold
Undisturbed, unfound, unsold
Awaits the coming of the dredge
To yield it from its rocky ledge
So they might find and weigh and measure
And then assay their new-found treasure.

Heated, melted, purified
Molded, polished, glorified.

The goldsmith works and does his duty
Creates in it a thing of beauty.

In the stream of life
    amid the throng
Lie glittering nuggets
    all along
Awaiting all across the land
For the touch of The Goldsmith's hand.

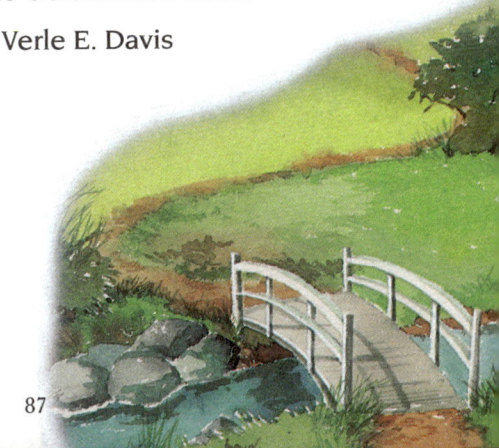

                Verle E. Davis

Perhaps

Perhaps the rain will fall today
    And spoil the plans we've made.
The clouds may chase the sun away
    Or dampen our parade.

Perhaps today a tear will fall
    As teardrops often do
When unforeseen the heartaches call
    And take a toll on you.

Perhaps these things shall come to pass
    For life goes up and down,
But God shall send you greener grass
    When yours has turned to brown.

For every drop of rain that falls
    A flower somewhere grows
As seasons change and time recalls
    The beauty of the rose.

        Clay Harrison

Imagery

Today I saw a robin,
And my heart began to sing,
For I know the little robin
Is a sign of early spring.

With my imagination
As vivid as it can be,
Suddenly it is spring again
In all her gaiety!

The trees are green and stately,
It is my steadfast belief
God again has resurrected
Every single little leaf.

Red roses climb the trellis,
I can hear the mocker's trills,
The flower beds are picturesque
With tulips and daffodils.

But my imagination
Tends to run away with me,
And with spring close as the robin,
I must await -- reality!

    Laura Baker Haynes

Fellow Travelers

Today I take your hand,
Tomorrow you may need mine;
We share in one great love,
The love of the Divine.

Today I soothe your brow,
Tomorrow you'll comfort me,
We have a common bond,
It's called humanity.

    Dorothy Niederberger

Thank God for Little Things

Thank You, God, for little things
    that often come our way,
The things we take for granted
    but don't mention when we pray,
The unexpected courtesy,
    the thoughtful, kindly deed,
A hand reached out to help us
    in the time of sudden need -
Oh make us more aware, dear God,
    of little daily graces
That come to us with "sweet surprise"
    from never-dreamed-of places.

      Helen Steiner Rice

Used with permission of
The Helen Steiner Rice Foundation
Cincinnati, OH 45202

Symbols

God helps those who help things grow
With seeds of kindness...that they sow.
For those who serve Him...every day
Unselfishly...in some small way,
His blessings pour out...our reward.
We are the vessels... of the Lord.

Our gardens grow...our fields will flourish
For every soul...we help to nourish.
Growing...stretching...reaching out
To those in need...and those who doubt.
We are...extensions...of His love,
His hand...holds tightly...to our glove.

By our good works...and each kind deed
We manifest...His name...His creed.
Then mortals...such as you and I
Are Symbols...here to glorify.
With a cheerful heart...that gladly gives
We prove to all...that Jesus lives.

            Patience Allison Hartbauer

A Yellow Daffodil

Oh, the glowing beauty
    Of a yellow daffodil,
Bringing springtime freshness
    To a winter window sill.

Like a living promise
    Of garden, song and sun,
Joyous little prelude
    Of the lovely days to come.

Like a note of laughter
    Upon a dreary day,
Breaking through the winter's gloom
    With melodies of May.

Strange how notes of beauty
    Can change our world about,
Bits of loveliness in life
    We cannot do without.

Oh, the loving kindness
    Of God whose sovereign will
Could pause to make, for you
    And me, a yellow daffodil.

            Alice Hansche Mortenson

A Balanced Life

My life has been balanced
    with pleasures and trials,
I've had many teardrops
    and thousands of smiles.
I've soared to the moon
    and I've plunged to the sand,
My life has been balanced
    by God's loving hand.
I've had many friendships
    I've had a few foes,
In the life of a Christian
    that's the way that it goes.
Should I just accept
    only good from God's hands?
No, I must endure
    whatever He plans.
But I can be sure
    and you can be, too,
All things work for best
    as God deals with you.

        Betty Purser Patten

This Life Is What We Make It

Let's oft'ner talk of noble deeds,
And rarer of the bad ones,
And sing about our happy days,
And none about the sad ones.
We were not made to fret and sigh,
And when grief sleeps to wake it;
Bright happiness is standing by—
This life is what we make it.

Let's find the sunny side of men,
Or be believers in it;
A light there is in every soul
That takes the pains to win it.
Oh! there's a slumbering good to all,
And we perchance may wake it;
Our hands contain the magic wand—
This life is what we make it.

Then here's to those whose loving hearts
Shed light and joy about them!
Thanks be to them for countless gems
We ne'er had known without them.
Oh! this should be a happy world
To all who may partake it;
The fault's our own, if it is not—
This life is what we make it.

Faith to See Me Through

Lord, grant me now a good night's rest,
A respite from day's work.
The burdens have been heavy;
You know. I prayed. You heard.
At times I thought I could not go
A step past where I was,
But You were there to guide me, Lord,
To help me tread the dust.

Lord, grant me now a good night's sleep,
The morrow comes so soon.
New tasks arise, new burdens press
Before ev'n comes the noon.
So many problems, unresolved,
Will greet the morrow, too;
Lord, grant me Your beloved sleep...
Then faith to see me through.

Loise Pinkerton Fritz

My Farm

My farm to me is not just land
Where bare, unpainted buildings stand.
To me my farm is nothing less
Than all created loveliness.

My farm is not where I must soil
My hands in endless, dreary toil,
But where, through seed and swelling pod,
I've learned to walk and talk with God.

My farm to me is not a place
Outmoded by a modern race.
I like to think I just see less
Of evil, greed and selfishness.

My farm's not lonely, for all day
I hear my children shout and play,
And here, when age comes, free from fears.
I'll live again, long joyous years.

My farm's a heaven, here dwells rest,
Security and happiness.
Whate'er befalls the world outside
Here faith and hope and love abide.

And so my farm is not just land
Where bare, unpainted buildings stand.
To me my farm is nothing less
Than all God's hoarded loveliness.

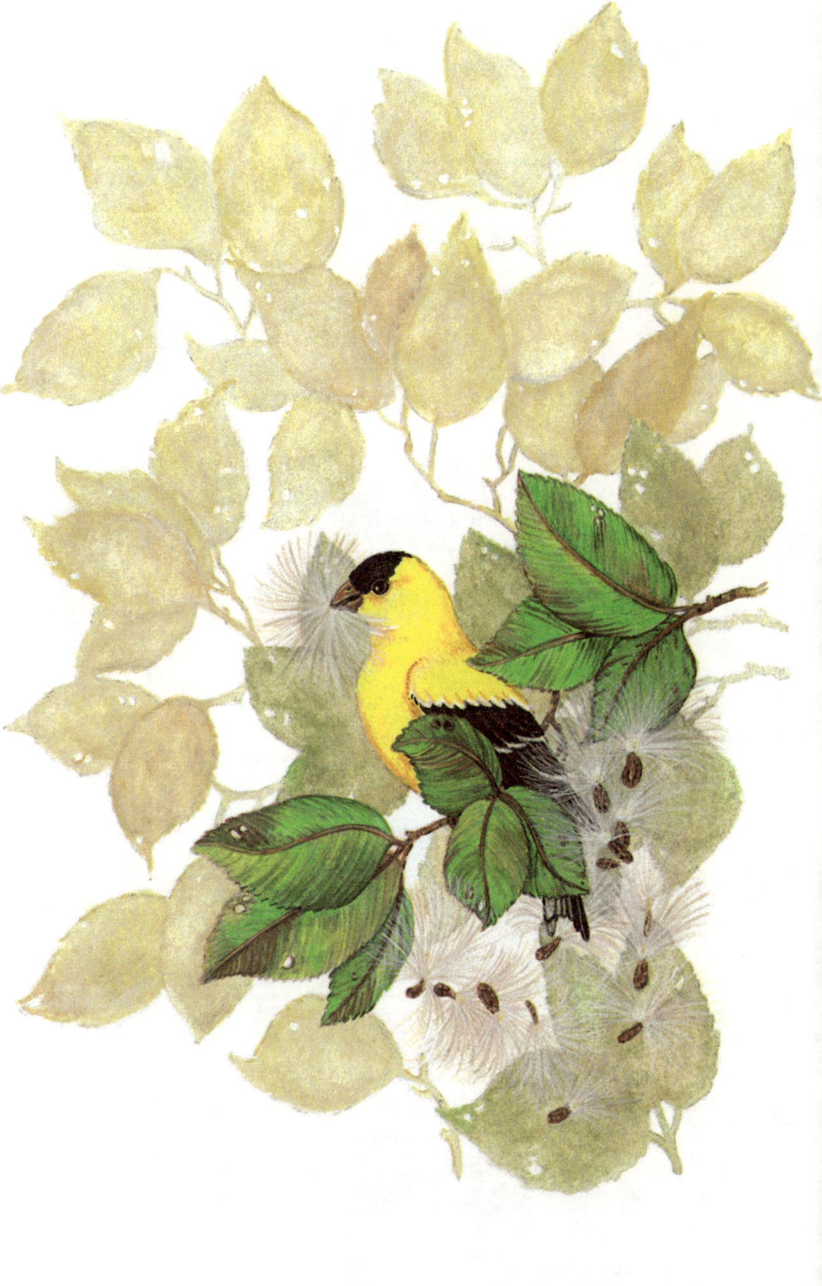

Show of Faith

Faith, in God, must show itself
    In deeds we do, each day -
By acts of kindness, love and care,
    That mark the Christian way;
It's not enough that we profess
    To hold to Christian views,
We must show faith, throughout each day,
    In everything we do.

In search of goals and dreams of life,
    We must pursue His wills
And be of service, unto Him,
    Until our life is stilled
For, when He lifts our souls, to judge -
    Above the realms of earth -
By deeds of faith, we leave behind,
    He will decide their worth.

                Michael Dubina

Living the Word

Folks go to church on Sunday,
And think they "have it made,"
But there are six more days in which
To practice what we've prayed.
You can't just read the Scriptures,
You have to live them, too,
And in your soul you must believe
God knows what's best for you.
Life takes a lot more giving,
Than most of us condone,
But everything belongs to God,
... And nothing is our own.

Grace E. Easley

My Treasures Are Secure

The treasures of this earth will perish,
    For they never can endure,
Safely in the arms of Jesus,
    All my treasures are secure.

The burdens of this life are many,
    But I try to wear a smile,
For when the load becomes too heavy,
    He will carry me a while.

Though I may be old and lonely,
    And earth's treasures may be few,
There's a mansion up in heaven,
    Loved ones there are waiting too.

Christ will give me strength and courage
    As I journey through the years,
And someday in heaven's glory,
    He will wipe away my tears.

When I walk the hills of glory,
    And I see the beauty there,
In the storehouse of the Father,
    Treasures far beyond compare.

        Gertrude B. McClain

The Miracle Of Spring

Oh, the glory of the springtime
    When bud and leaf and flower
Awaken to the call of life...
    The Resurrector's Power;
Revived from months of winter sleep,
    The early blossoms ring
Their floral bells in joyous praise,
    And sing the song of spring;
Hallelujah, winter's over!
    Renewed is life on earth,
Behold, the miracle of spring,
    God's Promise of rebirth!

          Dorothy M. Cahoon

Season of Rebirth

Peeking through the window pane,
A robin joyously
Sang a tender sweet refrain
To tell me it was spring.
Although white patches everywhere
Still lay upon the ground,
Showy flowers, here and there
In clusters could be found,
And bursting buds, on shrub and tree
Seemed anxious to display
Their fragile springtime finery
To all without delay.
It was the season of rebirth
That God sends in the spring,
When flowers start to bloom again
And robins come to sing.

    Elsie Natalie Brady

Great Faith That Smiles is Born of Great Trials

It's easy to say "In God we trust"
When life is radiant and fair,
But the test of faith is only found
When there are burdens to bear –
For our claim to faith in the "sunshine"
Is really no faith at all,
For when roads are smooth and days are bright
Our need for God is so small,
And no one discovers the fullness
Or the greatness of God's love
Unless they have walked in the "darkness"
With only a light from above –
For the faith to endure whatever comes
Is born of sorrow and trials,
And strengthened only by discipline
And nurtured by self denials –
So be not disheartened by troubles,
For trials are the "building blocks"
On which to erect a fortress of faith
Secure on God's "ageless rocks."

Helen Steiner Rice

Used with permission of
The Helen Steiner Rice Foundation
Cincinnati, OH 45202

A Poet's Prayer

Let me not lose the wonder of
    this earth
When I become enmeshed in daily
    toil.
Open my ears to Springtime's
    joyous mirth,
My eyes behold the promise of
    the soil.
Let me remember quiet mountain
    heights,
Or dusk who folds her wings above
    the sea.
Awake to crystal dawn's first
    freshening lights,
These things make life so beautiful
    for me.
Give me the faith to see beyond
    all fears,
And wisdom for each trial that
    meets my day.
Teach me the words to halt my
    brother's tears,
And find the courage in truth's
    shining way.
Of all my prayers, Lord, grant me
    this one part,
The understanding of a loving heart.

        Zelma S. Dennis

Gifts of Glory

I can see the gifts of glory
    God has willed to earth and man,
But their miracles of splendor
    I will never understand;
Works of majesty and wonder -
    That are everywhere I look -
From an ocean's wild enchantment
    To a peaceful, forest brook.

I can see a touch of Heaven
    In the flowers that He sowed
For they bear the awe of stardust
    And a twilight's afterglow.
Does not matter where I wander -
    Day or night, on land or sea -
Everywhere, I see the glories
    He has willed to earth and me.

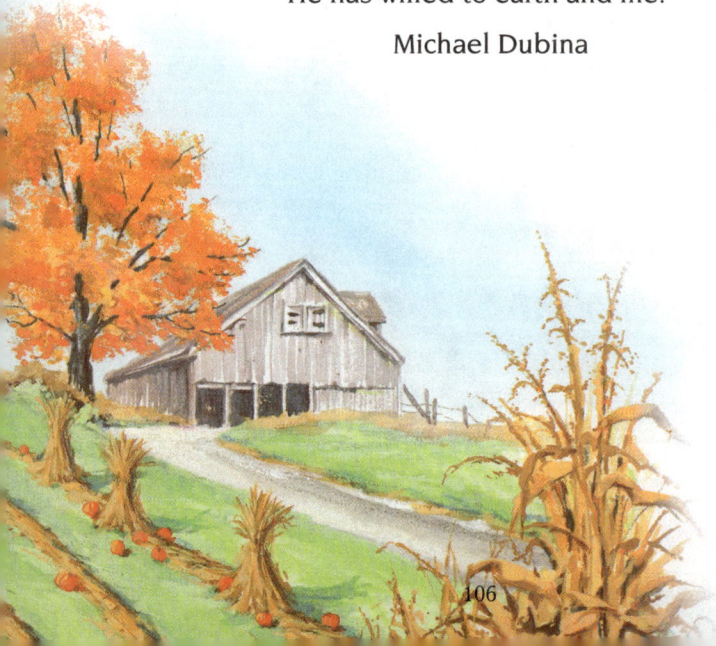

        Michael Dubina

Treasures of the Heart

My memories often wander
To those peaceful country lanes,
Where traces of my childhood
Bring a haunting, sweet refrain.

Times were grand, yet simple
(As childhood days should be),
And with each new tomorrow
Came a special joy for me.

To live again these moments
That occupy my heart,
Gives life a precious meaning
And each day a brand new start.

So when I find a need for
A happy thought or two,
I wander to my childhood
Where skies were always blue.

        Catherine Janssen Irwin

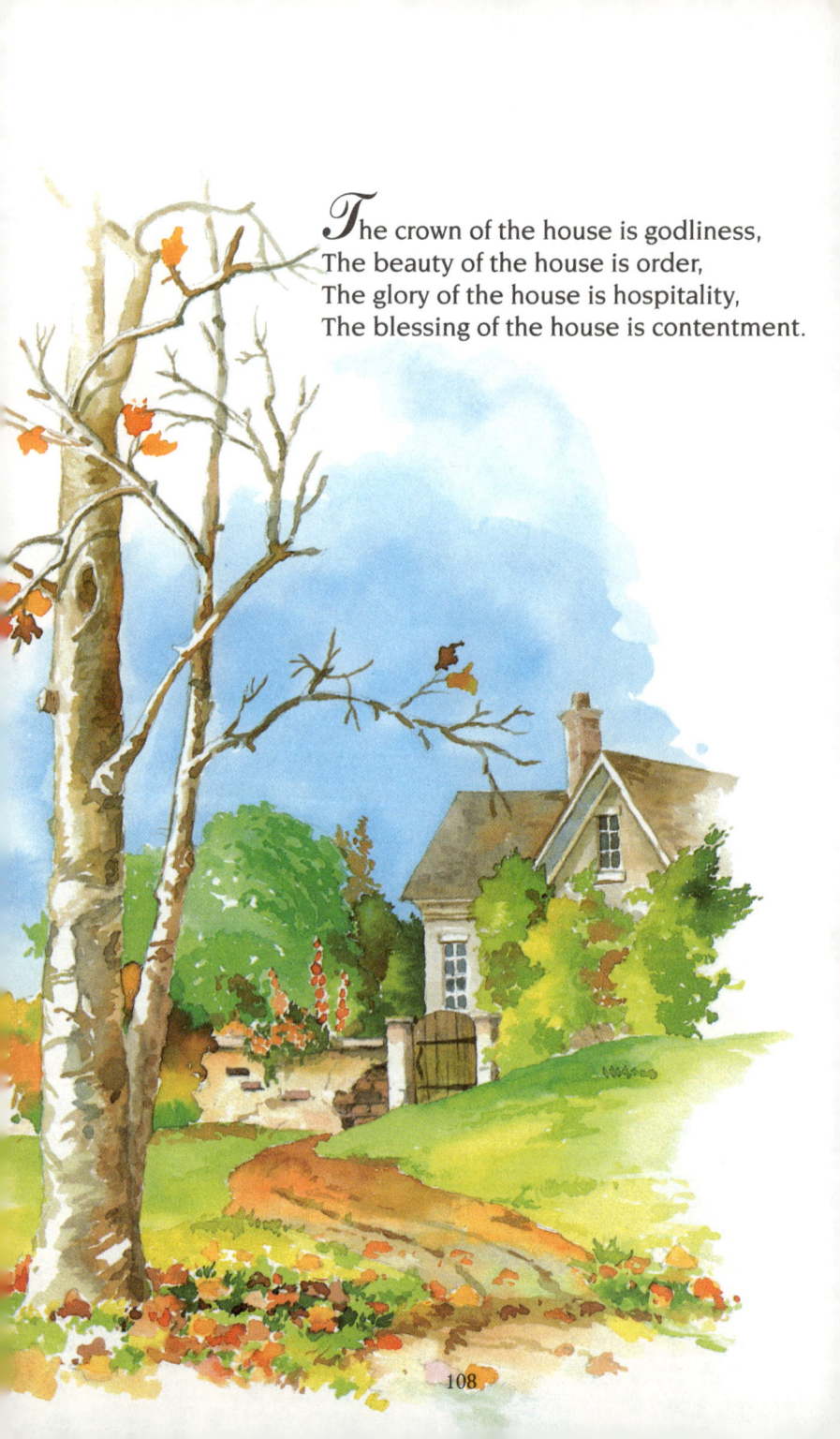

The crown of the house is godliness,
The beauty of the house is order,
The glory of the house is hospitality,
The blessing of the house is contentment.

The Sweetest Place

A home is a welcome refuge
From the stress and storms of life
Where the children love their mother
And a husband loves his wife.

A home is a hall for music,
For gay laughter, or repose,
A place to enjoy your hobbies,
To sing songs or plant a rose.

A home is a peaceful chapel
Where a family says its prayers,
It's a gym for recreation,
A retreat from business cares.

It's a school of good example
How to live and how to die,
It's the sweetest place I know of,
To your home does this apply?

        Sister Mary Gemma Brunke

Lips of mine, speak always well
Of others with the words you tell;
Eyes of mine, see only good
In others, as each Christian should;
Hands of mine, much can you do
To aid the weak that come to you;
Feet of mine, run swiftly on
As every loving deed is done;
Heart of mine, heed well the call
Of charity, which covers all;
Give love, as Jesus did command,
To the poor and weak of every land.

      Marion Schoeberlein

A Recipe For Living

A goodly bit of laughter
And a sky of fairest blue,
A touch of true believing
And a bit of humor too,
Some sunshine bright and golden
Yet a pinch of hurtful pain,
A morning kissed by dewdrops
Then an afternoon of rain.

Add a portion still of gladness
And a smile all soft and sweet,
A childish hug so precious
And a gentle dream complete,
Some teardrops mixed with problems
Then dilute them with a sigh,
Ever hope and faith to cling to
And a twinkle in an eye.

Mix them all with love and kindness
With a gentle heart that cares,
Quiet moments – peace and friendship
And some tender whispered prayers,
Some understanding always
And an outstretched helping hand,
You've a recipe for living
In this bright and glorious land.

                    Garnett Ann Schultz

The Homebody

I do not need to leave my home
  To see inspiring things
Deserving to be stored away
  In my rememberings.

I do not need to tour a land
  That's different than this -
My garden filled with lovely flowers
  Will give me perfect bliss.

As for the wonders of the world -
  If I had seen all seven,
I'm sure I'd feel, on coming home,
  That home was nearer heaven.

Claire (Rachel) Hartnett

Priceless

The Lord has blessed me richly
With gifts more precious than gold,
The love He's placed inside me
Can't be bought or sold.
The Lord has blessed me richly
Though my pocket's empty now,
I feel a certain gladness
A wealth that He endowed.
The Lord had blessed me richly
With children, spouse and friends,
My heart sings grateful praises
As days come to their ends.
The Lord has blessed me richly
And you'll be richer, too,
Just invite the Lord to walk along
And talk along with you.

        Janice Cortis Kasowski

I Call it God

Rainbows and roses
And tender green sod...
Some call it spring,
But I call it God!
Breathtaking sunsets
That melt in the sea...
It's only summer,
But it's Heaven to me.
Leaves gold and scarlet,
An acre of sheaves,
Remind me in autumn
Who created the leaves.
With blankets of snow
God covers the ground
So people will know
That He's still around.
He changes the seasons
With His staff and rod...
Some look for reasons
But I call it God!

           Clay Harrison

A Walk on the Beach

In the moonlight by the sea
    walking slowly in the sand
    leaving footprints there behind me
    in the dampened ocean land.

Then the movement of each wave
    washes them away
    making smooth the path to walk on
    like the start of each new day.

I turn and watch the surf
    rush away my lifely sign
    and at once a thought comes to me
    this was done by His design.

For the sand is like a soul
    in need of cleansing, to be pure,
    so I look up to the Heavens
    say a prayer and ask the cure.

Then I walk all night in joy
    at the marvel of the sea
    while it washes away my footprints,
    it does more than that for me.

                    Frank Cimino

The Answer

In the tiny petal
   of a tiny flower
      that grew from a tiny pod...

Is the miracle
   and the mystery
      of all creation and God!

Helen Steiner Rice

Used with permission of
The Helen Steiner Rice Foundation
Cincinnati, OH 45202

Old Friends

There are no friends like the old friends
    And none so good and true;
We greet them when we meet them
    As roses greet the dew.

No friends are dearer
    Though born of kindred mold
And while we prize the new ones
    We treasure more the old.

There are no friends like old friends
    Where'er we dwell or roam
In lands beyond the ocean
    Or near the bounds of home.

There are no friends like old friends
    To calm our frequent fears
When shadows fall and deepen
    Through life's declining years.

And when our faltering footsteps
    Approach the Great Divide
We'll long to meet the old friends
    Who wait on the other side.

It's A Beautiful World

It's a beautiful world we live in,
And a wonderful day and age,
Life's book holds tender moments,
Upon each shining page.
Each little teardrop cleanses,
And helps us understand,
There's wisdom in each trial,
And pardon in each plan!

It's a beautiful world we live in,
Old yet ever new,
And chances by the dozen,
To prove that we are true!
We find strength when we need it,
In many different ways,
And shadows by their contrast,
Illuminate our days.

It's a beautiful world we live in,
And though the way be long,
What tones of joy ring out within,
A simple, heartfelt song,
Tomorrow's promise lies ahead,
And faith to right each wrong.
My heart grows light as the darkness fades,
And I'm glad that I belong!

                        Grace E. Easley

Make Me Worthy

Won't bother You with trifles Lord,
About my cares and such,
Just wanted to say again today,
I love You very much.

Won't ask for things I shouldn't have,
Won't bother You with greed,
Won't ask for anything but love,
For this, dear God, I need.

First let me thank You for the care
You give me day by day,
The gentle hands You lead me with
Lest I should go astray.

The pain within Your loving eyes,
The crown of thorns You wore,
The awful shame You suffered when
My sins You gladly bore.

Oh, precious Father this my prayer
Forever more will be,
That someday I'll be worthy
Of the love You gave to me.

    Myrtle L. Johnson

A Purpose For Trials

From morning till night
And, too, past the light
There are rivers that we
  must cross...
Rivers of fears and
Rivers of tears
And rivers of greatest loss.

But whatever it be
That plagues you and me,
What rivers that we must ford,
They all work for good,
For He said they would...
To strengthen our faith in
  the Lord.

                Loise Pinkerton Fritz

(II *Corinthians* 1:8,9)

A Better Day

Though the clouds are dark around us,
And the skies are filled with gray,
God will give us faith and courage;
There will come a better day!

Though our hearts are heavy ladened,
God will guide us all the way --
He will send us hope and promise;
There will come a better day!

Though at times we lose the battle,
We can trust God and obey;
He will lead us on to victory --
There will come a better day!

Though we feel despair and sadness,
We can strive and dream and pray;
God will always be beside us,
And there will come a better day!

              Hope C. Oberhelman

The Gardener

God has shown me how to find
Joys of heart and peace of mind;
He has taught me how to grow
Loves of life, I pray to know:

> Take a seed, He said to me,
> (Of each joy you want to be)
> And embody it to grow
> (With the loves you pray to know)
> Then, endear it with your care,
> 'Till I make its vines to bear,
> And divide its fruitful ends
> With your neighbors and your friends.

>> Michael Dubina

My Search

I searched for God where folks are told --
In art renowned and shrines of old,
Cathedral spires, and hymns sublime,
Dramatic sermons, cultured rhyme --
In noble aims, bold saints of fame,
And all grand things that bear His Name.

I found God in the simple things --
In childlike faith that each day brings,
A baby's hand and mother's face,
A father's hug and mealtime grace --
In russet leaves, soft April showers,
A bluebird's trill, gold meadow flowers,
In humble prayer, real friendship shared,
And in the eyes of one who cared.

                Louise Pugh Corder

The Tapestry

If you could weave a tapestry
Of all mistakes you'd made,
A dismal failure it would prove
Of unattractive shade.

Then you'd ask God to grant your wish
And change the threads around
So there might be some loveliness
Where only knots are found.

Why did you lock your handiwork
Behind a closet door
Where it will lie in solitude,
Grown larger than before?

Just take that homespun tapestry,
Shake loose the musty folds,
And God will give you threads of faith
To weave in pinks and golds.

                    Norma Childress

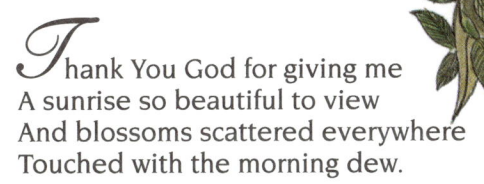

Thank You God for giving me
A sunrise so beautiful to view
And blossoms scattered everywhere
Touched with the morning dew.

Thank You God for friends to greet
And loved ones to share a hug,
For animals and birds that sing
And even a small lady-bug.

Thank You God for loving me
And for the gentle rain
For strength to smile at others
Even when I'm wracked with pain.

Thank You God for courage
To stand up for what is right
And to never let the devil
Even think he'll win the fight.

Thank You God for giving me
A sunset of brilliant gold
For a rainbow 'cross the eastern sky
So magnificent to behold.

Thank You God for everything
That comes along my way
For both happiness and sorrows
That fill my every day.

    Maryalice Friday

Thank You for the Gifts

Oh my Lord,
How little we
Appreciate the
Everlasting love
You bestow upon us.

How little we
Realize the many
Many gifts You
Give us to use.

How many times
We seek praise
From others for
Jobs well done,
Not remembering
That the talent
Came from You.

Forgive us, dear Father,
For our selfishness
And worldliness,
When the only praise
We need is Yours.

    Dona M. Maroney

Someone Cares

So many people need us
    Yet there be precious few;
To do the works of Jesus
    As He would have us do.

So many old and lonely
    Who hunger for a touch;
To let them know we love them
    And care so very much!

It doesn't take a mountain
    But just the little things;
Which warm the hearts of others
    To whom the Christ we bring.

Then let us share a rosebud
    And let us share a smile;
To help the sick and needy
    And make their lives worthwhile.

For when we think of others
    We think of Jesus too;
Who shows His love for mankind
    Through all good works we do!

Then let us not be backward
    As words of Christ we share;
Through gestures of compassion
    That all may know we care!

        Sancie Earman King

A Candle Wish

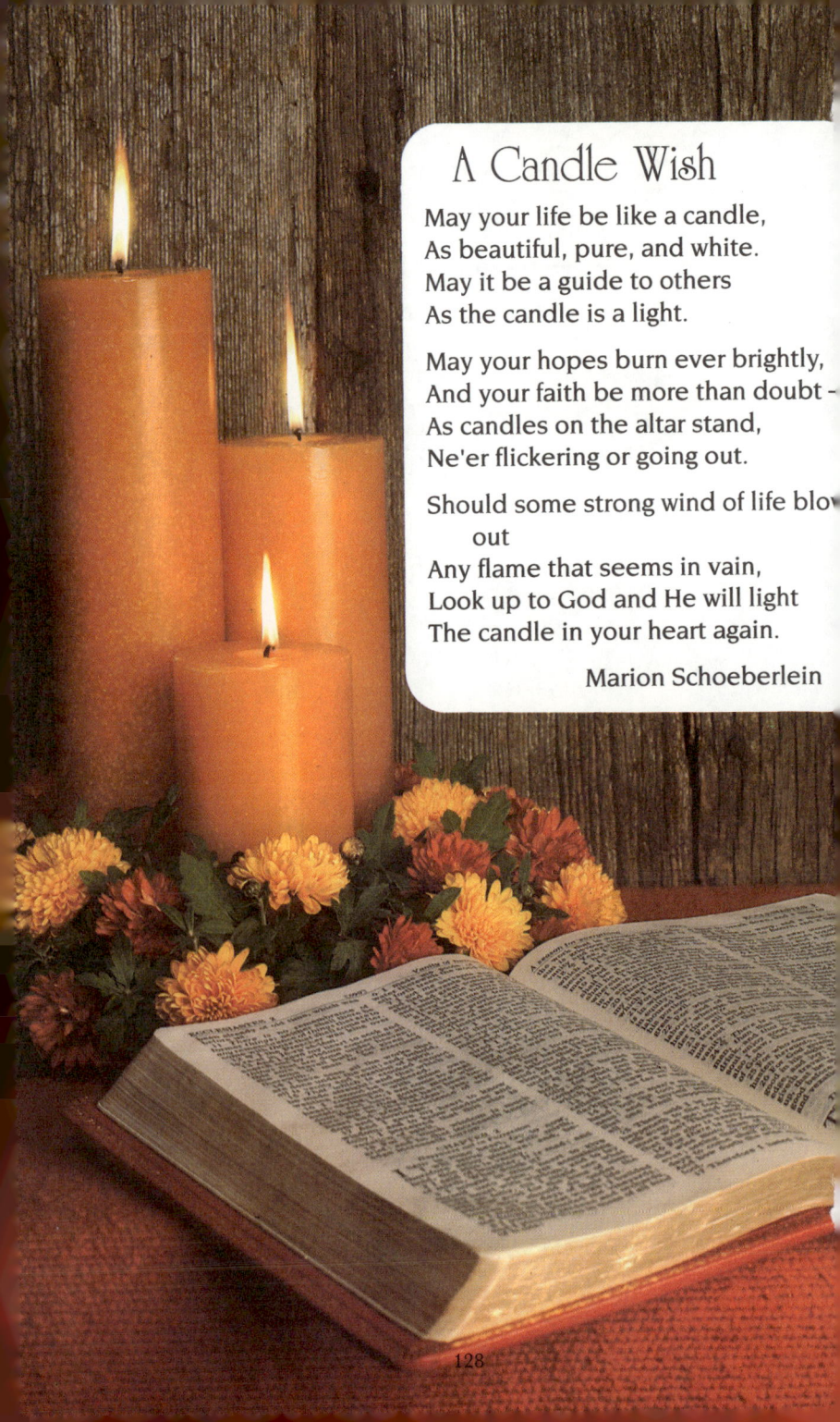

May your life be like a candle,
As beautiful, pure, and white.
May it be a guide to others
As the candle is a light.

May your hopes burn ever brightly,
And your faith be more than doubt –
As candles on the altar stand,
Ne'er flickering or going out.

Should some strong wind of life blow
    out
Any flame that seems in vain,
Look up to God and He will light
The candle in your heart again.

Marion Schoeberlein